The Spring Teller

Other books by the same author:

Poetry

Each Bright Eye
Bed of Stone
Tweed Journey
The Chanter's Tune
The Ringing Rock
The Lightning Tree

Non-fiction

Men and Beasts with Rebecca Marr, photographer

The Spring Teller

poems from the wells and springs of Scotland

VALERIE GILLIES

Luath Press Limited

EDINBURGH

www.luath.co.uk

First published 2008

ISBN (10): 1-906307-76-8
ISBN (13): 978-1-906307-76-9

The paper used in this book is acid-free, recyclable and
biodegradable. It is made from low-chlorine pulps produced in a
low-energy, low-emission manner from renewable forests.

The publisher acknowledges subsidy from

Scottish
Arts Council

towards the publication of this volume.

Printed and bound by
Exacta Print, Glasgow

Typeset in 10.5 point Sabon
Map © Ashworth Maps and Interpretation Ltd.
© Valerie Gillies 2008

for all fellow pilgrims along the way

Acknowledgements

For inspiration and friendship, I am grateful to Rebecca Marr, Walter Elliot, Roddy Mackenzie, the late Dolly Fraser, Elspeth King, Gill Fyfe, Patrick and Liz Maclean, Gus MacLeod, Carol Dunbar, Alistair Peebles, Anna S King, Chris Fleet, Angela Bourke, Cath McManus, Dilys Rose, Robert Alan Jamieson, Ted Bowman, Wendy Price, Larry Butler, Jennie Renton, my publisher Gavin MacDougall and the staff of Maggie's Centres nationwide.

Special gratitude is owed to Mick Ashworth for creating the poetic map.

For companionship on the journey, I would like to thank my husband William Gillies and all our family.

Writing this book would have been impossible without the Creative Scotland Award I received from the Scottish Arts Council: their panel understood the concept of a book of poems given by the springs and enabled me to go well-wandering.

Photographs by Valerie Gillies, Rebecca Marr, Anna S King and Alistair Peebles.

Contents

INTRODUCTION											15

HEALING WATERS
Earworm											25
The Eye Well											26
Three Clootie Wells
  1 St Mary's, Culloden Wood								27
  2 Munlochy											28
  3 Craigie Well										29
Writing on Water at Hart Fell Spa							30
Mans Well, Orkney										31

GUARDIANS
Frog Spring											35
The Green Well of Scotland								36
Honeybee, Inner Hebrides								37
Woolly Bear, Tinto Spring								38
The Butter Well										39
Tobar na h-Annait, Kilbride, Skye							40
Something's Happening									41
Source of the Tweed									42
The Spout Well, Applecross								43
The Westray Eel										44

KEEPERS
With the Well-keeper									47
Bernera Farm, Glen Elg									48
Samuel Rutherford									49
To Alexia											51
Craiglatch											52
Robert Burns' Mither at the Well							53
Heavenly Aqua										54

St Bernard's Mineral Well, Edinburgh   55
Washing the Saint   56
At Dolly Fraser's   57

KEEP WELL CLEAR
Monk's Well, St Andrews   61
The Balm Well   62
St Anthony's Well, Arthur's Seat   64
The World-Turtle   65
Resurgam, let me arise   66

LEGENDARY
The Wellhead   69
The Deil's Well   70
St Columba's Font Stone, Abriachan   71
The Well of the Outstretched Hand   72
Kilmory Oib, Knapdale   73
Mermaid Pool   74
Mine Howe, Orkney   75
It's the Pits That Make It   77
Queen Mary's Bath-House   79
Edinburgh Castle
    The Fore Well   80
    The Back Well   80
Brough of Deerness   81
St Wallach's Bath   82

NEW SPRINGS
Fiddler's Well   85
The New Spring   86
Slockavullin   87
The Moving Springs, Applecross   88
Frosty   89
The Goshawk   90
A Place Apart   91

TOPOPOEMS

Healing Well, Isle of Raasay 95
The Children's Well 95
Pictish Well, Burghead 95
Glen Mark 95
Chapel of Kilmore, Argyll 96
Robert Burns at the Brow Well 96
Tobar Ashik, Skye 96
St Bride's, Dunsyre 96

SEA, MEADOW, MOUNTAIN

The Sea-well, Bunchrew 99
Tobar na Slainte, Isle of Lismore 100
The Well o the Co, Mull of Galloway 101
St Medana's Well, Wigtownshire 102
Isle Maree 103
The Floating Stone 104
St Queran's 105
Brandy Well, Nick o the Balloch 106
Tobar a' Chinn, Corrie Vanoch 107
The Wells o the Rees 108
The Rant of the Names 109

IN IRELAND

St Ciaran's, Bavan, Kilcar 113
Gougane Barra, West Cork 114
Shandrum 115
Angels Well, Bindoo, Donegal 116
Myross Wood Grotto 117
St Bearchan's, Castlehaven 118
Well of the Holy Women, Teelin 119
The Well of the Winds 120
Gortaneadin Grotto, Inchigeelagh 121
Glencolmcille, Donegal 122
St Gobnait's, Ballyvourney 123

THE WELL AT THE WORLD'S END

Jambukeshvaram, India   127

Chamundi Hill, India   127

Lyssos, Crete   127

St Beuno's, Wales   128

The Mossy Well   129

MAP: SOURCES OF INSPIRATION   130

GAZETTEER: LOCATION OF SPRINGS AND WELLS   131

Photographs

FRONT COVER
The Spout Well, Applecross. Photograph by Valerie Gillies

BACK COVER
Mans Well, Birsay, Orkney. Photograph by Alistair Peebles

DEDICATION PAGE
St Columba's Font Stone, Abriachan. Photograph by Rebecca Marr

Photographic plates marking divisions of book:

HEALING WATERS
The Spout Well, Applecross. Photograph by Valerie Gillies

GUARDIANS
The Green Well of Scotland. Photograph by Valerie Gillies

KEEPERS
The Wishing Tree, Isle Maree. Photograph by Valerie Gillies

KEEP WELL CLEAR
St Anthony's Well, Edinburgh. Photograph by Anna S King

LEGENDARY
Kilmory Oib, Knapdale. Photograph by Valerie Gillies

NEW SPRINGS
The Fore Well, Edinburgh Castle. Photograph by Anna S King

TOPOPOEMS
The Back Well, Edinburgh Castle. Photograph by Anna S King

SEA, MEADOW, MOUNTAIN
St Queran's, Dumfries-shire. Photograph by Valerie Gillies

IN IRELAND
St Ciaran's, Kilcar, Donegal. Photograph by Valerie Gillies

THE WELL AT THE WORLD'S END
St Catherine's, Killybegs, Donegal. Photograph by Valerie Gillies

Introduction

I'M OFTEN TO be found with my head hanging over a drum of old masonry, or with my ear pressed to the ground, listening to the sound of a spring bubbling up to the surface. Other times I'll be lingering beside the outflow of a well into its stone basin or streambed, hearing the coded notes played by water.

What I can hear is the origin of sound and the tap-root of language. Springwater is like poetry, its source is underground.

In 2005 I received a Creative Scotland Award from the Scottish Arts Council to spend time travelling across Scotland, to write new poems inspired by the springs and wells. From thousands of these locations, I have chosen several to visit in different regions. Travelling to find them was often arduous, but I love the vast variety of wells and springs and the strangeness or the beauty of their locations.

What's a spring and what's a well? Springs bubble up and sometimes appear in new places: wells have a built stone tank or basin, and occasionally a medieval well-house or a stone canopy of some architectural interest. Domestic wells existed long before Scottish Water controlled our use of the element. Others are healing wells, visited by great numbers of people in the past and by many visitors today in search of a cure for every ailment from toothache to cancer. A well may have been famous for two thousand years and can still be active, frequented. Another may be neglected, a sad symbol of disregard in our urban deserts, waiting for our attitude to water to change: it may not have to wait too long.

My well-wandering began on a Sunday, the first in May, a traditional date for large numbers of people to visit the 'clootie wells' near Inverness and in the Black Isle, a tradition which is being revived. Perhaps this says something about the National Health Service. These 'rag wells' are popular as a place to go for a picnic and as a focus for ritual practised there. Leaving a rag at the well is done in the hope that the ailment or trouble will disappear as the cloth disintegrates. Beware of nylon! Pinning your synthetic fibres to the tree by the well might mean a protracted illness, one which takes longer to leave you because those materials take longer to decay...

Two tiny sisters, blonde pre-schoolers, told me how to approach the well of youth, where the water is meant to change into wine for a moment at daybreak. From that moment, it's true to say I've become more youthful, but then I am always seeking out wells and springs. Weatherbeaten, I have waded in my wellies through nettles and head-high cow-parsley. Hidden wells have led me down sump-breaker tracks and across ditches; I've gone leaping over bogs, untangling my hair from briars, snagging my worn breeks on barbed wire, dowsing with rods in flowery upland meadows or climbing wild mountain passes. I've picked blaeberries on the moors, brambles and raspberries in the hedgerows, and at last I've been rewarded with a sip of delicious water.

I've encountered the animal guardians of the wells who love to live around them. Two trout circle around with a yin-yang movement in a holy well in Argyll. Peregrine falcons soar above the well of the crag, ravens are vocalising near a cleft rock well. A herd of cattle follow me at the Butter Well. Spectacular dragonflies in Galloway, peacock butterflies in the city, the Scotch Argus and rare fritillaries fly near wells of the northwest coast. A honey-bee travels with us on the handrail of the yacht sailing to the spring near the beehive cells on one of the islands of the Garvellachs. Swift Arab mares and their foals graze near the source of the River Tweed. A redcoat roebuck drinks at a spring in the Pentland Hills during the drought. A golden frog lives at the spring by the watershed in the Durisdeer Pass. The biggest adder I've ever met guards the Green Well of Scotland with its hoard of sunken treasure.

Wells are sociable places, often visited quietly by locals, and by strangers too. Happy the man or woman who lives nearby and has the job of well-keeper, like Christine, the custodian of St Ronan's Wells, or John, the greenkeeper of the golf course who cleans out the Heavenly Aqua spring.

Traditionally many of our wells were thought of as sacred or holy, and there will likely be one close by where you live. Perhaps you will go to listen to it flowing, or if it is a silent one, to enjoy that deep silence. Perhaps you will want to adopt one, to care for it. Watching and listening at the well is our inheritance – go in search of yours tomorrow.

Making the pilgrimage to the well has been traditional for two thousand years, for which we have the evidence of the wells at the vast Roman fort and camps outside Melrose, filled with bronze face-masks and gifts of equipment. Healing wells are present across the country, like the Children's Well which cured whooping-cough. Tobar a' Chinn in Glen Isla cured rickety youngsters. Scotlandwell is reputed to have cured King Robert the Bruce of a skin disease. The Dripping Well in the cave at Craigiehowe cured deafness before the days of cochlear implants.

No-one can write the poetry of wells without visiting the Irish ones. I made two field trips: to the southwest, in Cork and Kerry, and to the northwest, in Donegal. Ireland was where it all came together somehow. I saw the Scottish springs and wells in a new light. I looked at some of the busiest and most famous sites, such as Gougane Barra, where there was a great midsummer pilgrimage to an island in Gougane Lake. Then I observed some of the more remote and hidden ones, such as Angels Well, Donegal, which isn't even marked on the map, but where locals gladly became my guides. The people of Ireland told me many stories of the search for healing and holy wells.

As I write, I have recorded over a hundred different wells and springs in my notebook, with digital photographs and sound recordings too, making a real archive and gazetteer. At all of these places I record their voice, their own sonic signature. From these sources I have composed poems in verse-forms as wide-ranging as the voices of the wells themselves.

It has taken a lifetime of writing about the elements and about locations for me to become poet enough to voice the nature of our springs and wells, to let them speak out. Each is like no other place on earth.

At several sites, usually urban, I have been asked to use the power of words to unlock a sealed or neglected well. One example is St Ninian's Well in the centre of Stirling, which used to be the town's water supply. It still flows today, in the darkness of its locked well-house, surrounded by car parks. By writing the poem, I became part of an initiative by citizens to revive a procession and open day for the well. Another example is the Monk's Well in St Andrews, which I came across in my lunch hour between school workshops. When I found that the well was being used as a trash-can, I composed a poem to read that evening at the StAnza festival. This has led to the well being cleaned out, given a sign, and visited by the schoolchildren. Events like this are reported in the national press under headings such as 'Well-Versed' and 'Who says poetry can't change the world?'

As the Edinburgh Makar, poet laureate to the city, I have used poetry to help towards restoring The Balm Well near Liberton, once an internationally famous well visited by pilgrims from all over Europe. With a history documented since the reign of Queen Margaret of Scotland almost a thousand years ago, it has been neglected in the last half-century, but now the local community intend to look after it in a more fitting manner.

The Spring Teller is moving into the future, both through this unlocking with words, and through writing workshops which I have designed to give people some of the tools associated with the healing wells, for use in their own fields of interest. The project has grown on a grand scale. I continue to write and to travel to the springs and wells, learning the lore surrounding them and the cures sought at them.

Many have been very difficult to find. Asking for help brings a generous response from locals, an exchange of stories, often an invitation to visit their own favourite spring.

People will give you all manner of reasons for visiting the wells: for health, for jobs, for a house, for a loyal partner, for fertility. Prayers of request, of gratitude, all are received by the well. If pressed, people will say that this is a place which is closer to some fourth dimension, to something greater than ourselves, to the saint who blessed it, to the other world, to the creator spirit. We hear something of our origin in its sound, and we come closer to finding the phenomenon of inner peace.

Valerie Gillies

for thirst
there are wells, springs, streams

for friendship
I have you, creator
of the white jasmine

Mahadeviyakka,
India, 12th century

Healing Waters

The Spout Well, Applecross

Earworm

Before the implant can help deaf people hear
Before the electrode winds into the cochlea
You lie below the cavern's crackpot roof
Letting the drop dripping from the rock
Fall first in one ear then the other

Getting an earful of cold in the interior
An earworm tune going round and round
As the ear is formed by sound for sound
To let you stand up and balance, to let
You hear the padfoot of your own footstep.

The Eye Well

Born blind in one eye, when your good one
was threatened, your mother upped and carried you
around the wells of Ireland: the wee girl
douking and dipping your head in pools
as if for apples.
                          At one overgrown place
she cleared away the grass and nettles
to wash your eyes in a pellucid spring.
It wept for you. And you peeped out
towards sky and trees recorded on the surface

with the eye-baby appearing in the centre,
your own diminutive reflection eye to eye
returning your long look. The wise water
kept getting clearer as you watched. Today

your good eye sees far more than most.

Three Clootie Wells
for Roddy Mackenzie

1 St Mary's, Culloden Wood

Let the wandering begin here, at the well of youth
As night turns to day on the first Sunday in May
When the water becomes wine, for an instant. At first sight
A rag well with its crop of cloots, its colours always afloat
And airy above ground, seems a mango-tope with odd fruit,
Golden orioles glancing through the grove, a strange tropic.

In the old birch wood, thickets of rags are tapestries
Of ribbons, designer logo bows, baseball caps and mossy socks.
Tiny sisters, two blonde preschoolers, will show you how
To silver the water with a coin, to wish and keep it secret.
I tied up my baby blanket last year. I can tie knots!
Smaller and wiser than you. Leave a rag, lay trouble aside.

Winding wool around, stringing up J-cloths and mittens,
A throng are tying their pain up, each illness and circumstance:
As the nurse says of her patients, *You have to get to the knot.*
The story in the yarn tightens the cord of the universe.
When you look back, only one rag stirs, casting the colours
In the wood of silence and stillness. It's waving goodbye.

2 Munlochy

The trees stand knotting their neckties at the well's mirror,
in the deep dark sound of its water.
A pale young man is making three circuits
of the Hill o Hurdie, against the stream of crowds.
A Ross County sports jersey is strung between two trees
– the old hanging god.
T-shirts wrap trunks with marker messages:
I love you Big Time.
Black-clad teenage boys put up knee-pads like hardened skin,
bend under rag-laden boughs

where sickness and suffering hang and no-one touches those or
lets them brush against them.
Synthetic trainers dangle by a lace, grow slime green.
Women hook a branch with a crook for yellow dusters: *There's
your cloot frae last year, Jessie!*
No more room on this one! A wealthy matron,
Mercedes-borne, straddles the stream,
flicks her silk scarf to one side
and drinks – *Ah, delicious!*
A child leaves a poem written to the place.

A tiny doll hangs by the throat at the black well-mouth.
The weak thin young man descends, takes water from the trough,
and puts it on his chest. His wife seals that with a kiss.
He wears his hospital wristband.
People are getting over everything,
using these rip-rag gallows trees.
Flying between the traffic, the rags are filled with lost bodies
and as the wind blows it out, look, there's someone in the shirt!

3 Craigie Well

The well has a gurgling voice midway between man and bird
as the dawn wave of willow warblers ripples through the trees.
Hearing this spring is how they learnt their song as nestlings,
with the cadence of soft liquid notes, a lisping *hoo-eet*,
not loud but clear and carrying far into the distance.
So youngsters take into their being the sounds of May morning.

Round and down to the well on skiddy stones, new planks,
two little brothers in red tracksuits tie up their cloots,
take a sip and make their wish, everything done in order.
their mouths fill with water and with laughter.
A briar bush is clad in the coolest threads,
the spring is a bird slipping out of its nest.

Tobar Chragag, well of the little rock,
Craiguch, Craigack, Craigie, Craigie,
chuckling, the chattering one,
chaffing, the laughing one
escaping into the sun,
joy live with you, Craigie!

Writing on Water at Hart Fell Spa

You can say anything to water. It listens better,
Closer to you than you are yourself. A word can begin
Its travels on the pool, can carry on to the river

From this spa, iron-rich and rising, reddening again.
Show a word to the water, reverse the lettering,
The motto quickens as the water takes it in.

A floating mirror reflects upon your writing.
What is above becomes what is below.
Carve a heart in the roof, the pool is beating.

A ray of light upon the surface helps to show
Where women once had recourse. To this spa
Their wheel-spokes turned, rolled in ironbound felloes –

Whoa now for the powerful tonic, a daily pint of salts,
And for the word above the water, mirror-writing mark.
Behind the wooden palings where the gully halts

Under the overhang, you are in Scotland's heart.
Green copper dots the rock in the half-dark,
The *forward* stream towards the future starts.

Mans Well, Orkney

Rumours of its healing powers have grown
ever since it washed St Magnus' bones.
Folk flock to it today, new patients
who say the water has eased their pain.

A neighbour leaves a cup at the spring,
a pyrex mug on a wooden peg
for the pure taste. A good strong flow
through the orange pipe and out it goes

beyond the well-strand, past yellow
marsh-marigolds to the working watermill.
In the grimmelins of a summer night
the spring is suffused with heavenly light.

grimmelins: Orcadian for twilight

Guardians

The Green Well of Scotland

Frog Spring

Surprised by my tasting the spring, a golden frog
leaps to the bank. He flies to froggy places,
his ankle-joints stretch the moment.

A puddock from his pop-eyes to his paddle-toes,
he darts out of the vital pool. Immortal frog,
to see him so healthy is a sure sign

the spring will do the same for me.
He hops past my shoulder into the paddy-pipes,
the reed-bed pockets frog. He vanishes through,
each spear of rush keeps its own drop of dew.

The Green Well of Scotland

is a dragon-hoard, where once the wily Dr Dodds brought ore
from the gold-wells of Cairnsmore to mint West Indian coins,
then hid from the law, throwing his apparatus and the money
into this deep quarry-hole that has no outlet stream, only
something experimental boils up that breaks the glassy surface
with a low puff and fuffing.
                    From her sunning-spot
among the rocks an adder speaks her hissy *whihe* sound
with her big yellow mouth. Coils as thick as your wrist.
Red eyes draw a bead on you. Three forehead scales
are gold coins. She's going to the water to drink.
As she slips away, her impetus is all in her head.

Honeybee, Inner Hebrides

We sail to the Garvellachs with an autumn wind
along the string of islands. Heading out over the waves,
a honeybee lands on the guardrail of the yacht.
Ginger-brown and banded, he is a lost forager

who travels with us, resting to regain strength.
Where the gap is navigable, we put in at a place
of sheltered creek and grassy hollow. A few steps
and we drink at the miraculous well of sweet water

dashed by salt spray. The beehive cells nearby
are circles of stone, overlapping slabs, a domed roof.
It takes a whole rocky island to make a single drop
of honey. How far to fly? A solitary bee arrives

who grips the hazel-rod rim of a coracle, till he flies
up and off rapidly, to find the golden honeycomb.

Woolly Bear, Tinto Spring

Woolly, woolly bear
Who feeds on the weeds,
Hurry furry chestnut,
Move at speed.

Wee hairy wobat
Warming in the sun,
On curlywurly loops
Many feet run.

By dandelion and nettle
Wriggly-squiggly crawl,
When you are touched
Curl up in a ball.

Woolly, woolly bear,
Ginger-beer froth,
Vanish and change
Into a tiger moth.

wobat: Scots for woolly bear caterpillar

The Butter Well

Cattle are gathering
to help me check it out
when thunder cuts our curds
skimming us off
the dish of the open field.

The plunger plumps down
in the sky churn:
I run with the herd
downhill, turn our hinders
to the storm sluice.

Bull, cows and calves
stamp their pattern
on a pat of butter
slapped and shaped
by clappers and water.

Tobar na h-Annait, Kilbride, Skye

Collie-paws splatter the car with mud.
Biddy, they're looking for the well.
Yes, it's there but it's boggy, very very boggy!

Tobar na h-Annait is a spreading dub
full of wild iris. Cattle pleuter in the mire.
It needs cleared and flows slowly.

In this fertile strath among the big bens
the Skye people wheezed on their way
to drink out of the horn of a living cow.

We're being watched by a cushy-cow,
a one-horned speckled cow who lows to us –
and nobody sees her go.

Something's Happening

At the Horse Well
the galloping hooves
come closer

the closer you get
the clearer they sound
so do the calls of the rider

Move away from the well –
the hoofbeats tap fainter
and fainter till they die away

in a steam-valve warning
a wind-speed feedback –
going to be a killer storm

Source of the Tweed

for Vivien

You asked me to give
a name to the foal
I thought of so many
you've kept them all

to give every year
to each filly or colt
who listens in the valley
for a name to be called

where they come cantering
mist lifts from the hill
your endurance champions
with speed and the will

to cross marsh or drumlin
moor or sand dune
your Arabs the poems
my words on the wind

The Spout Well, Applecross

The coastal well boasts its original ladle;
a fresh-faced woman drives a bottleful
hundreds of miles for a sick friend.

The holy well itself is set back
further from the road, in dense birchwood
where a guardian fly whirrs his psalm,

waiting for the day when his creator
will whistle for the fly that lives
at the sources of the streams of Egypt.

The Westray Eel

Cleaning out the well twice a year,
she puts a ramper of a fat yellow eel
into a tub of water for his ark.

Wide-mouthed and elongated,
he could set off through the dewy grass
for the Sargasso spawning-grounds.

But once he's put back in again,
the eel is so fond of his well,
he sits inside it and looks out.

Keepers

The Wishing Tree, Isle Maree

With the Well-keeper

At the Cleikum ceremonies a young boy
dressed in white as St Ronan
tosses two doves up into the night sky.
They fan out into blackness.

The boy drinks the water, too.
So many springs on this hillside.
Children eat sweets at the procession.
Lovers find a white feather at their dawn window.

The well-keeper gives a warm handshake.
The water tastes of sulphur, smells of gunpowder
and there's a tremor in those fingers
that fill and take a bottle away.

Youths of seventeen and eighteen
keep coming to sip at the white source.
Lately they've been found
kneeling on the steps.

Bernera Farm, Glen Elg

Bernera, the glen of the gap,
is opening a break in space:
the spring full as a cup-mark
in its cylindrical concrete casing.
Now Anne MacRae has gone
with her brown blessed hand
that smelt of oiled rolled fleeces
and kept the well clean,
the trout, the guardian of the spring
has gone too, has disappeared.

The setting summer sun will light
on another young redhaired Anne
who wanders beside the hazel wood
below Cnoc a' Chomh-ruidh,
the rock of the running-together,
not long before her wedding.
She only has to gaze
beneath the surface for there to be
green and gold, with fine speckles,
a rare trout circling for a moment
revealing himself to her alone,
life-giving, boundary-crossing,
the fish in the well.

Samuel Rutherford

(1600–1661)
the saint of the covenant

On warm summer evenings
the children would look down the shaft
of the village draw-well
to watch the water springing up.

One little fair boy, on impulse,
leaned towards the universe
in the well where bubbles
scud across like comets.

Face-first he toppled over,
his limbs poured into its cup.
The others ran home for help
crying how he'd gone down.

The well took everything, even
the screech of his fall.
Cold rose up his spine
as he sank quickly,

kicking while water dragged.
No handhold on the bald wall,
he was pulled under, spun
around, he looked up

to where someone was climbing
over the top and coming down
alongside him. Streamers
flashed off his shoulders

as he held the boy's chin
above water, bringing him
up to the top past the scars
of old floods on the wall.

All the way up, light
orbited the well. Tipped over
the rim, the wet boy sat,
took each breath as his first.

He opened his eyes wide,
saw his mother hurrying to ask
how he got out. *A bonny white man
came and drew me out of the well.*

So they said an angel
dipped in, feathers and all,
to gather the child up
from the chasm on strong wings.

Samuel grew up honest,
of a hot and fiery temper,
free from ambition:
he became a famous preacher.

He would utter *a kind of skreigh,
you never heard the like...
you'd think he could have flown
out of the pulpit any time.*

To Alexia

You stretch out your arms to me as I leave.
When you can walk further, I promise we'll go
together to the well in the field where I'll show
you how to keep it clear: a white quartz pebble
we'll give it, and a rhyme round as an egg.
A bright blue light on the wing, a kingfisher will fly
and the well-eye will open to your blue-green eyes.

Craiglatch
near Clovenfords

On Saturday, a young man brought an old woman
– a terrible colour – to sit in the car.
He fetched her a plastic cup and she drank.
That'll do you good.

That's what I'm hoping, it's why I'm here.

Beeholes in the drystane dyke,
the only ones in the Borders,
face south to the sun.

And to think,
when we first came here,
we boiled the water.

Robert Burns' Mither at the Well
Grant's Braes, East Lothian

Ah'm gaun tae the well
wi my stoups,
hummin a sang.
Mony words, muckle drouth.

Ah mind anither well
ayont the braes
years an years back
the length o Alloway.

Ma bairn at knee-hicht,
he wisna twa year auld,
paidlin in the well-strand,
crawin gey bauld.

He gied a first seuch
o fontal words
that flowed sae free,
like ony bird.

A clear mouth has aye
its well-heid.
Puir lad, he's awa
whaur the well's niver dry.

Heavenly Aqua

The low sun strikes with shattered light
across the tractor. Brimmed with gold,
his head looks as if he's wearing a halo.
'If I'd kent ye were comin I'd have
cleaned it oot for ye. It's no much
tae look at noo, it's all ochre. If I pour it
intae my whisky, it turns it green.'
A screed of rainbow oils on the surface
runs out of a D-basin, with waving
growths like oranges or Tibetan curds.
Dip a finger, it smells of rusty railings,
tastes of their corrugations. At the centre
of the moor is this heaven-sent chalybeate
whose iron in the water turns tea blue.

St Bernard's Mineral Well, Edinburgh

Wedding-parties eddy by
in little shoals for their photographs.

An athletic statue on the rotunda,
the goddess of Health carries her urn,
a serpent spiralling up to drink.

Damp mosaic in the pump-room:
visitors pack in, they keep swinging
the worn red-bronze handle.

The valves clack on an airlock,
no water from the lion's mouth.

A bubble-headed boy runs in,
shakes hands with the pump-handle:
the full force pours out.

Washing the Saint

At the far end of the grass-grown path
I clean out the well, lift twigs away.

The water popples and rushes clear:
a cloud adrift in it, a head of silver hair.

An old woman always kept this well;
she washed the image of the saint each year,

bathing the wood, wiping him clean
lovingly, she rinsed him again

to give these rinsings out for cures.
Fumac, wild crazy saint of Botriphnie,

dressed in green tartan, on your knees
you crawled and shuffled round the parish

to protect your people from disease.
A bent hawthorn with its creamy may.

Flung away downstream, your image
was broken up and burnt like a heretic.

Rain sprinkles the surface of the pool,
yellow flag iris and the blue begin to bud.

The outflow runs below a granite spar,
first ripples shimmer their stream joy.

How did it take so long to find you?
A trickle of light graces the wet meadow.

At Dolly Fraser's

Her head and face light up
to tell us of the Silver Well,
'It's a cold cold well, icy cold.'

The big map spreads over
her tiny lap like a flowery skirt.

'As children we had to put on
our boots to go down there.
It's marshy, there are always adders.

We all drank it if we were ill
because it was so good.'

Healthy at nearly a hundred,
Dolly's eye holds a gleam
of the purest water.

Keep Well Clear

St Anthony's Well, Edinburgh

Monk's Well, St Andrews

On a spot looking out over the surf
grows a grassy knoll with a round roof,

this is the wellhouse a monk built,
whaleback of slabs and a flag lintel.

Stone steps lead spiralling down.
where water still trickles within the mound

it oozes out to a widening ripple
promising healing and renewal

till its mouth is choked by a gag of litter:
irnbru cans, plastic bottles, fag-end fritters.

Who comes here to the holy well?
Three students arrive for a smoke, they tell

how they thought it was just another tomb
used by truants as a smoking room.

Thank you for letting us know what it is.
All three in long black overcoats, St Cainnech's

new community founded beside the well.
It drips once or twice in its simple cell

dissed-dissed, dissed-dissed.
It needs to be cleaned out and rinsed.

Between virid walls that stink of smoke
here is the spoilheap of our hopes:

somehow fresh water will flow to us yet,
two drops at a time, *res-pect, res-pect.*

The Balm Well
Saint Catherine's Balm Well, Edinburgh

'fons cui olei guttae innatant scatturit ea vi'
Hector Boece, *Scotorum Historiae*, 1527

*'This fontane rais throw ane drop of Sanct Katrine's oulie, quilk
was brocht out of Monte Sinai fra her sepulture to Sanct Margaret,
the blissed queen of Scotland... This oulie has ane singulare vertew
agains all maner of cankir and skawis.'* trans. Bellenden, 1536

Tell us about this dirty puddle outside the pub,
With its scum of petrol greasy to the touch?
– It took one drop spilt from the phial
Carried from Sinai to Scotland, to make the well
Burst out here. The saint's balm has oozed

Through centuries of use, *a kind of black fatnesse*
To smear on scab and skaw and itch,
All troubles of the human skin. For every
Aching bone, and against asthma or insanity
This was the tarry remedy, the brimstone balsam.

A tiny spring through the oil-shales below
Sends a slick of oil to swim upon the surface,
A creamer separating cream from milk.
the queen founded her chapel by it, vanished now;
Renaissance doctors analysed its grease.

A king made a flight of steps for easy access,
Fieldworkers stored its ointment through the year.
Cromwell's soldiers, camped on the Galachlaw,
Tore its stones down. Repaired afterwards,
The sovereign remedy still seeps out the wall.

Under its old fleur-de-lys finial, this evening,
Children at play have placed on the lintel
Cherry-blossoms and grasses, freshly plucked.
They peer through the padlocked grille at the chamber
Where the rest-level of the water lies at well-top;

They spy its bottle of black cloud, coating
The arch over with bitumen, treacle in a tin.
Strange angel gloss, divine oil-duct,
Streaked with its coal-tar antiseptic,
Glib iridescence curves in blue and purple

Smelling of coal-smoke, hot creosote.
Tar in a pot. See the sides weep the way
Tears run down a human face. The gathering
Balm is breathing through the air
For this is where our nation first struck oil.

St Anthony's Well, Arthur's Seat

How to rescue the old well?
Today a young man and his girl

climb together around Haggis Knowe
by its cockleshell black basalt brow

to raise a laugh, to rouse the echo
of young folk coming to the outflow

who washed their faces, two by two,
and made a wish in May-day dew.

The girl jumps up to sit astride
the dome of a boulder brought by ice.

It bears the cosmos like a pack:
a turtle carries the girl on its back.

A grey-green face the spring reveals.
The copper pipe is capped and sealed

where newborn waters once would rise
to wet a bandage for a child's eyes,

where humankind might hope to dwell,
the turtle-head withdraws into its shell.

The World-Turtle
for St Anthony's Well, Arthur's Seat

They had no right
to seal up the well.
A great grey boulder
tries to drink
out of the stone basin.

When the world heats up
the turtle who carries
the universe upon its shell
will turn over
and die of thirst.

Resurgam, let me arise
for St Ninian's Well, Stirling

Poor old well, once the town's main water-supply
but boarded up, it still bubbles pure and clear
in the cellar of the wash-house. Try the key,
some WD40 oil, a screwdriver, to open up
the long draw-bolts and padlock. The metal door
swings back, a fleet sound greets the torch.
Here's the flow that reared the cottagers' children
like young trout fry,

                    speckles playing with the stream.
Under the new car park, it sounds below the road-roar,
a trickling lade breathes and chafes against blackness.
Shackles are on air and water, transparency is trapped
and song shut up. St Ninian set prisoners of war free,
burst lock and chain. Let these fetters fall away,
release the well into the day for all to see.

Legendary

Kilmory Oib, Knapdale

The Wellhead
to the Scottish Parliament

Right by the gate where you go in and out
there's a well of tradition, your *tobar an dualchais*,
a carrying stream towards a kist o riches,
the street-well close by Queensberry house.
Water-pipes channelled through the living rock
supply the city, spring-fed from the hills,
a conch through which your ancestors sing and talk.
Those water-caddies of the Old Town come to fill
their wooden churns bobbing on an iron hoop,
pay fines for flyting and scolding, jump the queue,
bring clear water to the houses in a stoup
and the sough o an auld sang for a lanely youth.
You never miss the water till the well runs dry:
our young people at a loss, without knowing why.

The Deil's Well

Dinnae tell whaur it is –
ane o satan's satellites
wi his daurk sun ablow the yird.

Aabody's feart their name's hackit
ontae a sclate and drappit in
lettin the tow gang wi the bucket.

He's aye guid tae his ain:
an ill wish gangs doon within its waws
like butter in the black dug's hawse.

St Columba's Font Stone, Abriachan

The heart-shaped rock holds a hollow,
A bullaun-full of rain in the shape of a bowl.
Fresh water is always found in it, they say,
Even in the hottest weather, filling the cavity.
A small opening in the rock, a blow-hole

Spouts the spiracle of life from its poll
So close to me, in with my marrow
Which is lucky to be alive and well happy
The heart-shaped rock holds a hollow.

At its centre, a round reservoir, the sole
Drink women in childbirth would swallow.
A bottle brimmed here for baptisms, yesterday.
Mica flashes in the schist, shines reflectively
Into the O of antiphon, of fontanelle, the whole
Of the heart-shaped rock holds a hollow.

The Well of the Outstretched Hand
for Rebecca Marr, photographer

Massed thunderclouds storm along Loch Ness.

We turn into the dense wood, put it on like a coat
for shelter. We've come a long way for this well.
Hunkered down, Rebecca is drinking from cupped hands
when I see something white cresting the bank
to shake a glossy fern above her raven hair.

The ghost swift moth is flying out of the wood,
maybe, whose hindwings flash brightly.
Or the sun splashing the roadside hedge-parsley,
these foamy flowerheads. Or uncurling fronds
of mist rise above the rill, this white hand

hovering over whoever drinks, to share the light.

Kilmory Oib, Knapdale

Walking a path of close green turf in the goldcrests' forest,
he finds a cross-slab standing by the well among ruined houses.
On the slab carved birds perch, and under the curved
armpits of the cross the discs of sun and moon roll on.

In this sequestered place he'll stop for water to brew up.
Stepping-stones in the wet. A level crop of peppery watercress.
A stone-lined tank of moving clarity is carrying
a freshwater shrimp, two water-boatmen, a pale blue worm

folding and unfolding on its way. Purple heads
of self-heal rise above the clearing where he says aloud
a prayer in Gaelic for the people of Scotland.
All of a sudden the well blows one great bubble,

the air from below ground belling in response,
Kilmory Oib! the one voice left in the deserted village.

Mermaid Pool

she's married to the farmer here
the wet edge of her apron betrays

how she loves to swim in the river
every day around noon

a naiad with no clothes on
a glimmering body of water

a whiteness swimming up
out of the deep pool on the bend

blonde tresses braid the current
her slit ears half-way in water

her soap-suds are the foam
on the reaches below Dod Mill

keep looking into the pool
and you will see her

but if she sees you first
she can take you with her

Mine Howe, Orkney
for Alistair Peebles, photographer

We are going into the pict-mirk.
We let ourselves down backwards
holding onto a little thread
of light on the spiral stairway
that leads to the innermost darkness.

With shaky steps, toehold on treads,
the torch useless, our shoulders jam
against the walls, a pebble rolls
down past our hard hats
and rumbles into the hole below.

We hover on the half-landing
where a dog-skull guarded
the branching side-chambers.
One by one we enter the well.
Here's bodyroom enough for two,

a beehive chamber where we are held
in Mammy's Howe, the womb-house
with its neat channel drain for
the world-flood to pour away.
It's all around us.

You climb back up to the surface
and call down. If I can hear
your question I must answer.
My hollow howe-speaking
mouth spouts off oracles,

tapping the spring to prophesy,
to find a way to avoid disaster.
From all the islands people came
here to the oracle, they made it
so that we could become it.

The stair is a rush of warm air.
From the howe-dumb-dead depth
drawn up the flight of steps
comes the sibyl, so withered
in the jar, only her voice is left.

It's the Pits that Make It
for the Trimontium Trust, Newstead

The Well Meadow won't lie fallow, the ploughland
Is speckled with pits, a field freckled with new shoots:
Over a hundred hidden wells sealed with clay stopping,
All air excluded. Pillars of earth send down taproots.

Underworld-dark, they lead away, out of sight.
Suspended shapes are shining in the soil. There –
Look! A blaze of light coming up from the pit wall.
Golden yellow, brass. Red glaze, Samian ware.

The earth's gate opens. This is the lined well
Down which the oak-staved Roman bucket drops.
Their place on the Via Trimontina is the showcase
For their camp kettles, big jars, cooking pots,

Adjustable padded helmets, earpiece and face mask,
And for legionaries who make it to the end,
Medal backing-discs and saddle-horn stiffeners,
Someone's hat of hair moss. It's the stuff of legend.

For anyone who ever scratched his name,
A *graffito* on a white bronze cup says *Maximus*.
An iron handle marks *the property of Niger*.
Dometius Atticus and *Lucanus* too have left us.

Our own names lead the march by a phalanx
Of men wearing headsets, *Gucci* sunglasses, overalls
From *Beyond Retro*, mesh vests by *Rokit*, *Galliano*
Hats, *Moschino* sandals. Shine on, robot metallers.

How can we value the instant flash of this faceplate
Visor against the flash of the world's steeliest eye-to-eye stare?
Or these bones and skulls of nine horses and the slender
Girl groom lying across the pit below them? A charioteer

Drives nine red horses over the heavens now.
For the well is the way to the other world, where a rattle
Sounds in the hiss of a sistrum, the beak of a raven
Barks, the waves thrash and the winds whistle.

Long-jawed hounds guard a Pompeii of the north.
A child's shoe in one piece of leather: the outpost of the dead
Is not far away. The leg-bone and spur of a cockerel:
For a moment we hear it crowing in the land of the shades.

Hazelnuts, the matter in a nutshell. A hazel twig
Freshly cut with a sharp tool, bright and silvery,
At the bottom of the well. What's sealed up is a mystery.
See the twig and long to see the whole tree.

Place of peaks and pits. Night soil and ritual rubbish,
Wells drawn into vanishing point. This remote outer
Edge of the earth, Trimontium, it's the pits that make it.
How deep it goes, our thirst for their first water.

After the rites are over, these are left for the hallowed well:
The water-filled cup, a splash of scarlet, the ceremonial flask.
A row of lights moving in the evening. The land herself
Holds a lamp and a battered helmet mask.

Queen Mary's Bath-House

Pom-pom
On the green,
A wee den
For Scotland's queen.

A fat turret,
Old oak peg,
A tall chimney
Like a leg.

A spring flows
Through the floor,
A golden dagger
In roof-boards.

Crown and castle,
Pot-belly hut,
Clootie dumpling
Boiling up.

Her changing-room
For tennis games
Long ago,
Just the same.

A spy-house
For looking down
On her garden
Beyond the town.

Pom-pom
Pompalary,
A play-house
For Queen Mary.

Edinburgh Castle
for Anna S King

The Fore Well

The swow of looking down
into this volume

an illusion striped across
with a black and white check

it becomes a highland plaid in thin air

the garrison saves snow for water
as the water-level drops

here their tartan floats

The Back Well

They live on salt herring
and dry bread.

I am the Back Well:
in a siege
depend on me

Brough of Deerness

Unseen, a loon wails with eerie call.
Mist swims on the sea. A nonstop knocking
taps from the cave-gorge of The Gloup,
that blow-hole in bad weather.

Fulmars pass within arm's length,
great skuas rob a black-backed gull
right in front of our eyes. Searching
for good health, we find the chapel well,

circle it in silence, throw two handfuls
of water over head and shoulders,
coorie in to nodding grasses on the cliff edge,
watch the globe curve round the horizon.

St Wallach's Bath

This old kirkyard by the River Deveron
is the same one Sileas looked down upon
from her pink-gold castle, with her great songs.
By midday the river pelts full and fast,
rushing through the cavity of the saint's bath
with grey-green waters clearer than glass.

Who would dream of bringing her child
down here, among rapids running wild
on an outing to the pools of swirl?
She'd need to heal the clouded lens of eyes
which are sore, unable to weep, always dry;
or to cure the child who never thrives.

Every year hundreds of children dipped
and hung up rag or shirt or bib
torn off their little bodies, with a pin
to be left in a pot-hole, milled ceaselessly
till the Deveron flooded both bath and tree
and swept all the offerings down to the sea.

New Springs

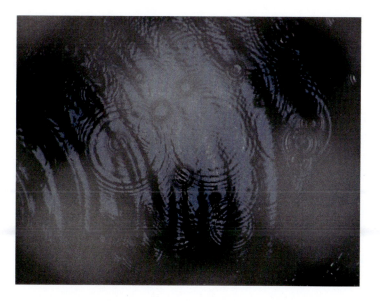

The Fore Well, Edinburgh Castle

Fiddler's Well

Two wind-blasted fir trees on the precipice edge.
The young man on the cliff path has left
his friend's funeral only an hour ago.
He walks through the rain, the sea far below.

At close range, a buff-tailed bumble-bee
shelters on the platform of a foxglove flower.
He sees its face, and hears a high-pitched whine,
bee wings vibrating with the voice of his friend,

amplifying it, *Dig, Willie, dig and drink!*
He scrapes barehanded in the steep bank.
His head is buzzing. A trickling runnel arrives
to cure his tuberculosis: he survives.

The New Spring

Tin-can traffic sours the inner city park
while hailstones go stotting off the grass.
A new source breaks out of the ground,
stirring up a dance of sand grains,
air snatched into water sparkles,
fed from the spring of all beginnings.
Small children run up to its brink,
draw the warm breath of the brae.

Slockavullin

Boys' laughter in the cottage
pauses, skips a beat.
Not a drop from the big pipe,
the perch for a scrubbing-brush.

An invisible music splashes
as it rises from deep inside
like trowie tunes, overheard
from within a fairy mound:

diddey-de da-dee da-diddey
diddey-dum de-dum de-diddey

The fiddler lifts the bow
smartly off the strings
in a Scots snap, plays a new tune,
the Slockavullin strathspey.

The Moving Springs, Applecross

On the slope the bubbling springs
burst out the top
of tumid mosses

highpitched helium voices rushing
those fast hussies
with lippy bubbles

make for the bay where porpoises
are rising to spout
ready to play

In a flat calm the explosive puffs
of blowing porpoises
continue

while they summer in the sound
their echo-locating
moving on like springs

Frosty

A pillar of mist is rising above the moor
as the hoarfrost hoists a seeding cloud

Springwater steams on a frosty morning
the white lady rustles her fabulous skirts

A snifter of vapour stoves out from the marsh
and rolls on in sworls where it meets the air

The white horse steps up from a sunken place
his green teeth reek, champing in your ear

The Goshawk

Searching through the wildwood
when you can't find anything
and you can't hear or see a spring

a goshawk swoops through the trees
in pursuit with dashing wingbeats

binocular eyes under a heavy brow
its face shoots forward orange-yellow

as it chases a young thrush
surprised by this ambush

manoeuvring with a hunting scream
between branch and branch the goshawk goes
those eyes take on a blood-red glow

A Place Apart

for the Quiet Room, Marie Curie Hospice,
Fairmilehead

Here is a quiet room where you can stay
And you do not need to say

Anything. Three windows look out east
Toward a distant coast that calls the geese.

One window holds the southern hills,
Moorfoots and Pentlands to wander at will.

This shelter-belt of trees is closer in
Where branches bend in every wind,

Birds can perch or take their flight,
And leaves can turn to face the light.

The high stars rise, wheeling by again
Above the deep stillness of the hill and glen

And only a moment ago a Scottish king
Came this way to the Balm Well's healing spring.

Topopoems

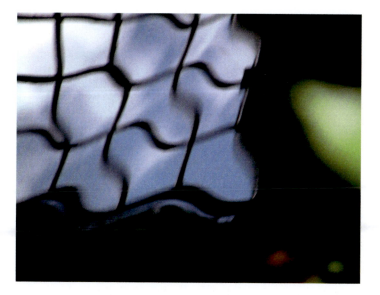

The Back Well, Edinburgh Castle

Healing Well, Isle of Raasay

Don't think about it,
don't look for it,
that's how you'll find it
without searching the mountain

The Children's Well

To learn the time
of sea-tides
the children watch the well
as it ebbs and flows

Pictish Well, Burghead

Massy on the headland
a spring-fed cistern
big enough
to swim a bull in

Glen Mark

A sapphire on the moor,
protruding from the glen's navel,
a gallus button winks up from the pool
in the centre of the bowl in the mountains

Chapel of Kilmore, Argyll

Walk up for a glimpse
of the two *mysticall fishes*:
the bow-waves of trout
hunting across the shallows

Robert Burns at the Brow Well

Suffering his last three weeks of fever,
he hoped to live, and drank from the *Bru*:
Burns seemed mortal then, he never knew
how mightily his hope was answered

Tobar Ashik, Skye

Bi glic! Bi glic! persist the oystercatchers;
Tobar Ashik absorbs our footsteps, grows quiet
as if it is listening, and recalling others from before:
after a moment or two, its clear sound flows on

St Bride's, Dunsyre

Drink and dream
how
Brigid hung her gown
on a sunbeam

Sea, Meadow, Mountain

St Queran's, Dumfries-shire

The Sea-well, Bunchrew

The sea-well went under the salt water
At high tides. It flowed so strongly
The cattle stood up to their hocks
To drink from its freshwater pocket.

Now trains bounce over subsiding tracks.
Low tide, wet clay at the spot.
Roll it in your hands,
They come away clean.

Tobar na Slainte, Isle of Lismore

Six knots, with red-brown sail,
G & T aboard, up the Lynn of Lorn.
Row ashore in the dinghy, wade
in wellies through the kelp
onto a slithery rocky shelf.
Hear water flowing, find the well
spurting right out of the ground
below a little limestone cliff.
Liz drinks to be rid of her cough,
has a long healing sleep
in the cabin later. Got anchor,
sailed north past Lilian's washing,
sheets flying in a freshening breeze.

The Well o the Co, Mull of Galloway

There is no spring; it is kept full by the surf
seething over the rocks at high tide. Cupped
in the cove, it waits on the ebb. Watch till the core
surges all by itself like the pool at Bethesda
pappling and sooming, the stirring-up of the water
where he will ask, *Do you want to be well?*

St Medana's Well, Wigtownshire

Medana left Ireland and the man
who stalked her. Stepping onto a rock,
she floated here across the bay.
He followed, tried again to praise her.
She plucked her own eyes out.
You want these? He left unseen.

A disc of blue, the spring is flowing
from the boat-shaped rock
and its strand enters the salt sea.
This is where she washed her face
and somehow she could see again:
the painful stabs of sea holly,

a rock pipit on the cliff,
its streaked breast.
A tight cluster of sea aster
and a great mass of thrift.
Two perfect quartz pebbles
white and smooth as eyeballs.

Isle Maree

To treat insanity, the patient was rowed
Sunwise round the island, tossed overboard
And roped in again three times, gasped
A wish and nailed a coin into the tree.
That well is dry, the dead tree thrust
Into its socket, a sharp mockcroc of coins
Bearing heads, protruding half-moons.
Bad luck will follow a stolen coin
Out onto the stormy loch, forcing
The boat's return to the stunted grove.

The Floating Stone

Wind-and-wave whinstone, a bleached snowshoe
With two hollows cut for a pair of bare feet:
Magnus sailed to the island on this floating stone.

The saint ran down with his surfboard to cross
The open waters of a dangerous firth. He left
Footprints our living feet can touch, thinskinned.

Farm children wonder when their peedie feet
Will match his. One size fits everyone grown.
We watch a big easterly sea running by

On the day a pod of orcas passes South Ronaldsay.
Travelling fast, a black dorsal fin tall as a saint
Breaches on the grey-white saddle of the whale.

peedie: Orcadian for small

St Queran's

A wonder as rare as a craig in a carse
is this well in a moss, whose water
rises clear through a bed of peat
to the white metal of the saint's face
in the circular shaft. People leave tokens,
scraps of ribbon, gewgaws, biro pens
on bushes shivered by a quickening breeze.
Cleared, hundreds of old coins were found:
the burnished French, the Irish pennies,
the hardheads and bodles of James VI,
thin papercuts as bright as new copper.

Hot against these visits, the Presbytery censured
two women 'for going in ane superstitious way
to fetch the waters', forced them to repent
in the body of the Kirk. Deep down, unquenched,
they stooped their knees and hearts to the well.

Brandy Well, Nick o the Balloch

the red-gold girl
sister to the tree
when she feeds the necklace to the well
the water enjoys it

Tobar a' Chinn, Corrie Vanoch

Going up to the corrie, I rip my thin breeks
on a snaggle-toothed barbed wire fence.
By the tug of this path the glen folk came
crowding with their rickety children for a cure.

Someone or something is watching me:
maybe I'm in the orbit of rifle sights
or of binoculars from a distant skyline,
or an eagle on wing above the mountain.

I look around to see who it can be.
Bottled-up, a purple orchid pouts its lower lip.
Toothy leaves of water avens nod their lanterns,
and cuckoo-flowers prick their round-lobed ears

On the slope above, the spring of springs
opens an eye, blinks through white chickweed.
The well of the head is talking, many voices
in one, speaking fluently all by itself.

The Wells o the Rees

Oldest, farthest, out of the way,
bare-skinned in their prehistory,
the Wells o the Rees, my dearies.

Three springs in stone cupboards,
ledges with a recess, the sheepfolds
shelter the fresh water.

There's wind in the mouth of the wells
and the women are lilting
on the high milking pasture,

from their airy realm of Craig Airie Fell
they are looking out over the world
beyond the Rig of the Eyes

to the distant glinting of the sea.
The Wells o the Rees, my dearies,
kegs for your bog-butter.

The Rant of the Names

a change in the Wine Well
a ruby-red drop of the Claret Well
the Brandy Well in the Nick o the Balloch
belongs to St Brendan
well happy

a kettle filled at the Tea Well
Parritch Well for wholesome breakfasts
just one drop of the Heavenly Aqua
will turn your whisky green
well-liked

hard water at the Snappy Well
a healing dream after Sleepy Well
a boy lets a white dove go
into the night above the Doo Well
well away

whistle of Canary Well
tickle of Whisker Well
bubbling up of the Popple Well
the Spout Well speaks out strongly
well said

a gleam in the gloom of Trout Well
Hart Fell Spa high in the hills
it's misty around White Mare's Well
people see white horses there
well worthwhile

the Brae Mou opens in the north
a slick on Tarry Well
ointment from the Balm Well
the Brow Well where Burns bathed
for well-being

a girl plucks a rose at Tamlane's Well
trailbikers swerve by Katiethirsty's
Tobar Ruaridh is not to be
found by searching
well nigh everywhere

ice cold of the Silver Well
iron tonic of the Red Well
the sky sees the Bluewell
all the slap of Painted Effie
pull on your wellies

the Cow's Eye gives you a look
go for a sip of the Well of Youth
may morning find you there
Finfan Wells! sing all their fountains
Fin fan frew fruid flow!

In Ireland

St Ciaran's, Kilcar, Donegal

St Ciaran's, Bavan, Kilcar

Though the bogland opens up
he is tucked into his shelter:
once a wild boar helped him
to build his makeshift hut.

Gougane Barra, West Cork

Lights shine all night on the island
And on the path, to help people do the rounds
In honour of St Finbar. Source of the Lee,
Your only place to be. The causeway runs out
Into the lake, a single swan preens its whiteness.

Coins have been plucked out of the tree
To let it live. Bright stream of the *slánán*,
Where bottles are filled with blackbird song.
Chill cell, whose dark dazzles. Prayers
Cell by cell fill the vault of each ribcage.

Bridegroom then bride arrive in fertile rain
To the sound of car radios. In its own self
The well is like nowhere else on earth.
Water kisses their mouths, intoxicates,
The strand repeats *this place, this space.*

Shandrum

On the slope of the swell
rises a dwelling
for the hidden banked fire
deep as desire

The spring furls away
a wick through waxy
jamjars, a votive candle
and a scallop shell

Underneath the earth
the grass of the heath
and the briars writhe
tangled dead and alive

A long stone basin
trenches the souterrain
Who'll go into the hill?
Who'll stand where it is holy?

Angels Well, Bindoo, Donegal

You've come so far to find it and then it's not
    on any map.
Ask the locals. The young mother at the farm says
    it's a bad road.

But halfway up the hill the white statue will
    let you know.
Look for the well-keeper's stone house. *O Patrick,*
    he keeps it.

Happy the man who lives where miracles
    take place.
A white rosebush by the well, a plastic ladle,
    a scooped wash stone.

The sky brushed with wisps of cirrus, a hinge
    of mile-long ailerons
Trail their flight-fins in the air over
    Blue Stack Mountains.

The seven smooth curing stones lie in a row
    on a ledge.
On May Eve the women will arrive here
    for healing,

Passing the stones round about their heads
    with raised arms
And their crooked elbows will become pinions
    while angels gather.

Myross Wood Grotto

To travel is our new form of ascetic practice.
We speed along the road from Clonakilty
Through a fierce squall of rain that causes the cars
Ahead to brake, an invisible force till it slashes us.

In Myross, Fr Brendan sets us on the path,
You have all the time in the world.
In the dell where frost never reaches,
Pink and white windflowers blow by our feet.

St Bearchan's, Castlehaven

As we're climbing the stile, an old man appears
from his camper van on the quay, hitching
long crutches to his arms, hobbling to us.

Our own ancient mariner, Old Devonian
shepherd and poet, holds us with story and rhyme.
We promise to tell him if we find the well.

Where the iron gate opens to the wood
lies an immersion pool with entrance and exit.
We follow the valley further along.

On the south bank an orange fishing float
pops up alongside a white football,
rosaries and medallions on the bush.

The well is a seeper from the rocks.
The tree overhead weeps vapour drops,
trickles a rainforest benison.

The stream flows by the Mass Rock,
a tumbled candle. Running back
through the storm we call out to him,

It's here right enough!

Well of the Holy Women, Teelin

From the bay, the fishermen
point out the well on the skyline.
They would lower their sails
as they passed it.
You'll find an ould gate,
there it is, up above.
Eyes of Irish blue
turn and look into mine.

Three sisters lived on this hillside
in modesty, sense, understanding,
who blessed the well here.
The storm clouds are rolling
over Slieve League and over these
waterworn stones and mass cards
and now over the knotted brown
sackcloth scapular I'm leaving
from when I was young,
giving it over to memory.

The Well of the Winds

A tricky place, this can be lucky
or unlucky, can influence the weather.
Scoop it clear with a scallop shell
and a fair wind will bring the boats home.
Tend it, replace the stones with a kiss
before the storm overwhelms the land,
the grassblade shaken by an unseen hand.

Gortaneadin Grotto, Inchigeelagh

With newfound power the waters hurled
when the young mother spoke to two girls,
giving them messages: her image moved
alive, detached, across this open moor.

Tongues of water issue from the slit
of the ravine. The driver of a car sits
silently in prayer. On an outcrop of the grotto
a child's lips *smile from heaven* in his photo.

Glencolmcille, Donegal

Strangers come here to make the long circuit of the glen
where its steep slope runs inland, drawing down the rain.
On the move, pilgrims will drink a sip of well water
and look through the holed stone to glimpse eternity.

I kneel in the wet hollow while a raven goes cronking over:
mountain and sky grow greater from the Place of the Knees.
To make three turns clockwise in the saint's flagstone bed
knocks shins, bruises ankles, presses the breast hard

by revolving: the stone pillow rattles beneath my head
and rocks me each time I surface looking skywards,
lips uttering prayers. Balancing, I face up the valley,

bare feet gripping the tippy Slab of Request: the mist
lifts from my heart. Strange, back in Scotland, pegging
out washing in a high wind, to feel so changed.

St Gobnait's, Ballyvourney

The path runs by rounds
past the stones,
through the grove
to the spring on the hilltop.
First effervescence,
each bubble a globe,
you are looking into
the well of yourself.

The Well at the World's End

St Catherine's, Killybegs, Donegal

Jambukeshvaram, India

At Siva's place, on the island in the river,
he takes the form of a lingam of water within water.

Chamundi Hill, India

After the mother of all springs on her mountain,
other waters will seem tasteless.

Lyssos, Crete

How to be healed was simple.
Welcomed by gentle *therapeutae*,
The sick came to bathe,
To feed the snakes a honeycake,
To sleep on the floor of the temple,
Waiting for the healing dream.

St Beuno's, Wales
for Gus MacLeod

After the thirty-day silent retreat
you were able to discern what to do:
you ran up the road in your swimming shorts
and plunged three times into St Beuno's pool.

It was baltic!

Everything felt very warm when you came out,
everything was welcoming you
into this worldly order
of watery brothers and sisters.

The Mossy Well

Who will I meet
on the path to the Mossy Well?
For where it is winding
there's no way of finding
the blue dragonfly
to flash like a jewel
far out in the clearing
hovering over the pool.

Where is the brindled beauty,
the moth who drinks the dew?
she drifts like a feather
out of sight altogether.
Silver in the birch-trees
or speckled on the hill,
the bird will come questing
for one who loves her still.

Green cushion of moss
by the winding pathway
for the skimmer, the darter,
the hawker, the chaser.
Sometimes in the sun
sometimes in the shade,
as ferns love this mossy place
so we love always.

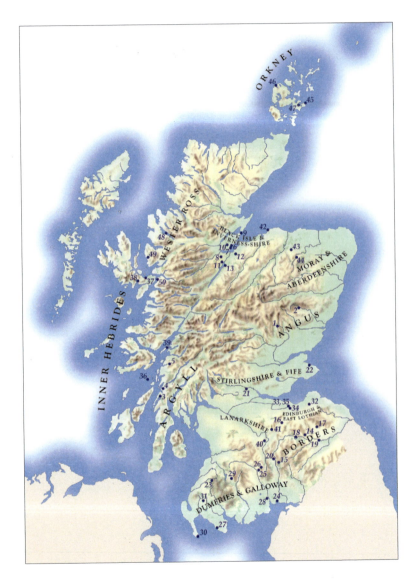

Sources of Inspiration

Map © Ashworth Maps and Interpretation Ltd.

Gazetteer
Locations of Springs and Wells

ANGUS
1 Tobar a' Chinn, Corrie Vanoch, Glen Isla, NO178620
2 Tobar na Gealaich, Glen Mark, NO419828

ARGYLL
3 Kilmory Oib, Knapdale, NR780902
4 Slockavullin, Kilmartin, NR825982
5 St Bean's, Chapel of Kilmore, NM887250

BLACK ISLE & INVERNESS-SHIRE
6 Craigie, near Avoch, NH679532
7 Dripping Well, Craigiehowe, NH685521
8 Dolly Fraser's, Muirton of Clunes, The Aird, NH552421
9 Fiddler's Well, Cromarty, NH808673
10 Munlochy Clootie Well, NH641537
11 St Columba's Font Stone, Abriachan, NH570347
12 St Mary's Well, Culloden Wood, NH723453
13 The Well of the Outstretched Hand, Loch Ness, NH576314

BORDERS
14 Craiglatch Spring, NT435373
15 Hart Fell Spa, near Moffat, NT097115
16 Heavenly Aqua, Rutherford Mains, NT164541
17 Mermaid Pool, Dod Mill, near Lauder, NT581480
18 St Ronan's, Innerleithen, NT328373
19 Trimontium South Annexe, Newstead, NT572343
20 Tweed's Well, NT053146

STIRLINGSHIRE & FIFE
21 St Ninian's, The Wellgreen, Stirling, NS796930
22 The Monk's Well, St Andrews, NO515166

DUMFRIES & GALLOWAY
23 Brandy Well, Nick o the Balloch, NX347924
24 Brow Well, NY085674

25 Butter Well, Muiryhill, NS877035
26 Spring, Durisdeer Lane, NS916059
27 St Medana's, Monreith Bay, NX364401
28 St Queran's, Troqueer, NX955722
29 The Green Well of Scotland, Carsphairn, NX557946
30 Well o the Co, Chapel Wells, Mull of Galloway, NX144315
31 Wells o the Rees, NX229724

EDINBURGH & EAST LOTHIAN
32 Robert Burns' Mither's Well, Grant's Braes, NT508724
33 St Anthony's Well, Holyrood Park, NT276737
34 The Balm Well, Liberton, NT273683
35 Wellhead, by the Scottish Parliament, NT267737

INNER HEBRIDES
36 Eileach an Naoimh, Garvellachs, NM639094
37 Tobar Ashik, Skye, NG687243
38 Tobar na h-Annait, Kilbride, Skye, NG589202
39 Tobar na Slainte, Lismore, NM872434

LANARKSHIRE
40 Spring, Tinto Hill, NS960356
41 St Bride's, Dunsyre, NT062478

MORAY & ABERDEENSHIRE
42 Pictish Well, Burghead, NJ109692
43 St Fumac's, Botriphnie, NJ376443
44 St Wallach's Baths, River Deveron, NJ427372

ORKNEY
45 Brough of Deerness, HY596088
46 Mans Well, HY256275
47 Mine Howe, HY513059

WESTER ROSS
48 Isle Maree, NG931724
49 The Spout Well, Applecross, NG716450
50 Well of the Trout, Bernera Farm, Glen Elg, NG808209

Luath Press Limited

committed to publishing well written books worth reading

LUATH PRESS takes its name from Robert Burns, whose little collie Luath (*Gael.*, swift or nimble) tripped up Jean Armour at a wedding and gave him the chance to speak to the woman who was to be his wife and the abiding love of his life. Burns called one of the 'Twa Dogs' Luath after Cuchullin's hunting dog in Ossian's *Fingal*.
Luath Press was established in 1981 in the heart of Burns country, and is now based a few steps up the road from Burns' first lodgings on Edinburgh's Royal Mile. Luath offers you distinctive writing with a hint of unexpected pleasures.

Most bookshops in the UK, the US, Canada, Australia, New Zealand and parts of Europe, either carry our books in stock or can order them for you. To order direct from us, please send a £sterling cheque, postal order, international money order or your credit card details (number, address of cardholder and expiry date) to us at the address below. Please add post and packing as follows: UK – £1.00 per delivery address; overseas surface mail – £2.50 per delivery address; overseas airmail – £3.50 for the first book to each delivery address, plus £1.00 for each additional book by airmail to the same address. If your order is a gift, we will happily enclose your card or message at no extra charge.

543/2 Castlehill
The Royal Mile
Edinburgh EH1 2ND
Scotland
Telephone: 0131 225 4326 (24 hours)
Fax: 0131 225 4324
email: sales@luath. co.uk
Website: www. luath.co.uk